Vegan Coo

Healthy And Delicious Vegan Recipes For Beginners

Copyright ©

All rights reserved. No part of this book may be reproduced, stored in a retrieval system, or transmitted in any form or by any means, electronic, mechanical, photocopying, recording, scanning, or otherwise, without the prior written permission of the publisher.

Disclaimer

All the material contained in this book is provided for educational and informational purposes only. No responsibility can be taken for any results or outcomes resulting from the use of this material.

While every attempt has been made to provide information that is both accurate and effective, the author does not assume any responsibility for the accuracy or use/misuse of this information.

Table of Contents

Chapter 1: Vegan Breakfast Recipes

Vegan Pancakes

Crepes

Apple Breakfast Cookies

Banana Breakfast Muffins

Vegan Tofu And Broccoli Quiche

Oatmeal Banana Breakfast Squares

Vegan Frittata

Avocado Breakfast Bowl

Banana Zucchini Muffins

Breakfast Skillet

Apple Pancakes

Vegan Waffles

Chapter 2: Vegan Lunch Recipes

Hot and Sour Soup

Corn Chowder

Beet And Carrot Salad

Black Bean Soup

Chickpea Skillet

Chunky Vegan Chili

Creamy Leek Soup

Vegan Bean Casserole

Quinoa Salad

Chapter 3: Vegan Dinner Recipes

Savory Cabbage Casserole

Tofu And Vegetable Peanut Stir Fry

Lentil Vegetable Bake

Eggplant And Zucchini Stew

Spicy Tofu Stir Fry

Spinach Casserole

Squash Stir Fry

Asian Tofu Stir-Fry

Slow Cooker Vegan Chili

Chapter 1: Vegan Breakfast Recipes

Vegan Pancakes

Ingredients

1 1/4 cups all-purpose flour

2 tablespoons white sugar

2 teaspoons baking powder

1/2 teaspoon salt

1 1/4 cups water

1 tablespoon oil

Directions

Sift the flour, sugar, baking powder, and salt into a large bowl. Whisk the water and oil together in a small bowl.

Make a well in the center of the dry ingredients, and pour in the wet. Stir just until blended; mixture will be lumpy.

Heat a lightly oiled griddle over medium-high heat. Drop batter by large spoonfuls onto the griddle, and cook until bubbles form and the edges are dry. Flip, and cook until browned on the other side. Repeat with remaining batter.

Crepes

Ingredients

1/2 cup soy milk

1/2 cup water

1/4 cup melted soy margarine

1 tablespoon turbinado sugar

2 tablespoons maple syrup

1 cup unbleached all-purpose flour

1/4 teaspoon salt

Directions

In a large mixing bowl, blend soy milk, water, 1/4 cup margarine, sugar, syrup, flour, and salt. Cover and chill the mixture for 2 hours.

Lightly grease a 5 to 6 inch skillet with some soy margarine. Heat the skillet until hot. Pour approximately 3 tablespoons batter into the skillet. Swirl to make the batter cover the skillet's bottom.

Cook until golden, flip and cook on opposite side.

Apple Breakfast Cookies

Ingredients

2 cups quinoa, cooked

2 cups rolled oats

1 cup brown rice flour

1 medium apple, diced

1 tbsp cinnamon

1/2 tbsp nutmeg

2 cups applesauce, unsweetened

2 tbsp vanilla extract

1/2 cup almond slices

1/2 cup walnut pieces

Directions

Preheat oven to 375F.

Cook 1 cup of dry quinoa in 2 cups of water and dice apple.

Mix together the quinoa, oats, flour, cinnamon, nutmeg, apple pieces, apple sauce and vanilla.

Drop dough on cookie sheets and use spoon to shape into circles. Top with the almonds and walnuts and bake for 20-25 minutes.

Let cookies stand for 10 minutes before transferring to the cookie rack to cool completely.

Banana Breakfast Muffins

Ingredients

3 cups all-purpose flour

1 cup white sugar

1/2 cup brown sugar

2 teaspoons ground cinnamon

2 teaspoons baking powder

1 teaspoon baking soda

1 teaspoon ground nutmeg

1 teaspoon salt

2 cups mashed ripe bananas

1 cup canola oil

1 cup coconut milk

Directions

Preheat oven to 350F. Grease 12 muffin cups or line with paper liners.

Mix flour, white sugar, brown sugar, cinnamon, baking powder, baking soda, nutmeg, and salt together in a large bowl. Stir bananas, canola oil, and coconut milk together in a separate bowl; mix banana mixture into flour mixture until just combined. Fill muffin cups with batter.

Bake in the preheated oven until a tooth pick inserted in the center of a muffin comes out clean, 30 to 35 minutes.

Vegan Tofu And Broccoli Quiche

Ingredients

1 (9 inch) unbaked 9 inch pie crust

1 pound broccoli, chopped

1 tablespoon olive oil

1 onion, finely chopped

4 cloves garlic, minced

1 pound firm tofu, drained

1/2 cup soy milk

1/4 teaspoon Dijon mustard

3/4 teaspoon salt

1/4 teaspoon ground nutmeg

1/2 teaspoon ground red pepper

black pepper to taste

1 tablespoon dried parsley

1/8 cup Parmesan flavor soy cheese

Directions

Preheat oven to 400F. Bake pie crust in preheated oven for 10 to 12 minutes.

Place broccoli in a steamer over 1 inch of boiling water, and cover. Cook until tender but still firm, about 2 to 6 minutes. Drain.

Heat oil in a large skillet over medium-high heat. Saute onion and garlic until golden. Stir in the cooked broccoli and heat through.

In a blender, combine tofu, soy milk, mustard, salt, nutmeg, ground red pepper, black pepper, parsley and Parmesan soy cheese; process until smooth. In a large bowl combine tofu mixture with broccoli mixture. Pour into pie crust.

Bake in preheated oven until quiche is set, 35 to 40 minutes. Allow to stand for at least 5 minutes before cutting.

Oatmeal Banana Breakfast Squares

Ingredients

3 cups oatmeal

1 cup unsweetened almond milk

1/2 cup agave

1/2 cup applesauce

2 mashed ripe bananas

2 tsp baking powder

1 tsp salt

1 tsp vanilla

1 tbsp cinnamon

Directions

Mix all ingredients and bake at 350F for 25 minutes in a greased 9 x 13 pan.

Vegan Frittata

Ingredients
1 cup raw spinach

4.5 ounces silken, extra firm tofu

2 tbsp. fat-free soymilk

1.5 tsp vegan egg replacer

1/4 tsp fresh thyme, crushed

Dash each of sea salt and fresh ground pepper

Directions
Heat oven to 350 degrees.

Lightly spray a small baking dish with olive oil or no stick spray and set aside.

Clean spinach and steam lightly.

Mash tofu in a small mixing bowl. Add thyme, salt and pepper and mix well.

Sprinkle egg replacer over mixture and mix well. Add soymilk and stir well.

Add steamed spinach and stir evenly. Place mixture into prepared oven dish, spread evenly.

Bake for 10-15 minutes, until lightly golden on top.

Avocado Breakfast Bowl

Ingredients

3 tablespoons olive oil, divided

1 (14 ounce) package extra-firm tofu, drained

1/2 teaspoon salt

black pepper to taste

1 1/2 teaspoons onion powder

1 1/2 teaspoons garlic powder

1/2 teaspoon ground turmeric

1 tablespoon fresh lemon juice

1 tablespoon olive oil

1 cup finely diced red onion

2 jalapeno peppers, seeded and chopped

1/2 teaspoon salt

3 cloves garlic, minced

2 cups chopped tomatoes

1 1/2 teaspoons cumin

1/4 cup chopped fresh cilantro

1 tablespoon fresh lemon juice

1 (15.5 ounce) can no-salt-added black beans, drained and rinsed

1 1/2 cups cooked hash brown potatoes

1 avocado - peeled, pitted and sliced

1 teaspoon fresh lemon juice

1/4 cup chopped fresh cilantro

1 teaspoon hot sauce, or to taste

Directions

Preheat a large, heavy skillet over medium-high heat. Add 2 tablespoons oil. Break tofu apart over skillet into bite-size pieces, sprinkle with salt and pepper, then cook, stirring frequently with a thin metal spatula, until liquid cooks out and tofu browns, about 10 minutes.

Be sure to get under the tofu when you stir, scraping the bottom of the pan where the good, crispy stuff is and keeping it from sticking.

Add onion and garlic powders, turmeric, juice, and remaining tablespoon oil and toss to coat. Cook 5 minutes more.

Preheat a heavy-bottomed saucepan over medium-high heat. Add oil. Cook onion and jalapenos with a pinch of salt, stirring, until translucent, about 5 minutes. Add garlic and cook, stirring, until fragrant, about 30 seconds.

Add tomatoes, cumin, and remaining salt, and cook, stirring, until tomatoes become saucy, about 5 minutes. Add cilantro and lemon juice. Let cilantro wilt in. Add beans and heat through, stirring occasionally, about 2 minutes. Taste for salt and seasoning.

Spoon some hash browns into each bowl, followed by a scoop of beans and a scoop of scramble. Top with avocado, a squeeze of fresh lemon juice, and a sprinkle of cilantro. Serve with hot sauce.

Banana Zucchini Muffins

Ingredients

2 1/3 cups grated zucchini

1 1/2 over-ripe bananas, mashed

1 cup applesauce

1 cup brown sugar

1/4 cup vegetable oil

1 tablespoon lemon juice

1 1/2 teaspoons vanilla extract

3 cups all-purpose flour

1 tablespoon baking soda

1 tablespoon ground cinnamon

2 teaspoons ground nutmeg

1 teaspoon baking powder

1 teaspoon salt

1/4 teaspoon ground cloves

1 tablespoon white sugar

1 teaspoon ground cinnamon

Directions

Preheat oven to 350 F. Grease or line 24 muffin cups with paper liners.

Combine zucchini, bananas, applesauce, brown sugar, oil, lemon juice, and vanilla extract together in a large bowl. Whisk flour, baking soda, 1 tablespoon cinnamon, nutmeg, baking powder, salt, and cloves together in a separate bowl.

Slowly add flour mixture to zucchini mixture while continuously stirring until batter is just combined. Spoon batter into prepared muffin cups about 3/4-full.

Mix white sugar and 1 teaspoon cinnamon together in a small bowl; sprinkle over batter.

Bake in the preheated oven until a toothpick inserted in the center of a muffin comes out clean, about 30 minutes.

Breakfast Skillet

Ingredients

2 cups frozen hash browns

1 cup chopped onion

1 cup chopped bell pepper

1 cup chopped broccoli

1 12-oz. package firm tofu, crumbled

2 tbsp nutritional Yeast

1/2 14-oz package vegan sausage, divided into 4 patties

Directions

Heat a large non-stick skillet to medium-high. Spray 1/2 of the skillet generously with cooking spray and add the hash browns. Divide the sausage into patties and add.

Once the potatoes begin to brown, add the onion and continue cooking 5-7 minutes. Flip the sausage patties.

Add bell pepper and broccoli, stir to ensure even cooking.

Save room on the opposite end of the skillet for the tofu. While the vegetables cook, crumble the tofu.

Spray the opposite end of the skillet with cooking spray, and add the tofu.

Sprinkle the tofu with the nutritional yeast. Scramble the tofu and yeast together to cook off any excess liquid.

Place 1/4 of the potato vegetable mixture on each plate then top with the tofu.

Season as desired.

Apple Pancakes

Ingredients

2 cups whole wheat flour

2 apples, peeled and cored

1 1/2 cups almond milk

1/2 cup coconut oil, melted

1/4 cup water

2 tablespoons baking powder

2 tablespoons cane sugar, or to taste

1 teaspoon ground nutmeg

1/2 teaspoon ground cinnamon

Directions

Blend flour, apples, almond milk, coconut oil, water, baking powder, cane sugar, nutmeg, and cinnamon in a blender until smooth.

Heat a non-stick griddle over medium-high heat. Drop batter by large spoonfuls onto the griddle and cook until bubbles form and the edges are dry, 3 to 4 minutes.

Flip and cook until browned on the other side, 2 to 3 minutes. Repeat with remaining batter.

Vegan Waffles

Ingredients

3 cups all-purpose flour

2 cups water

6 tablespoons coconut oil, melted

6 tablespoons white sugar

3 tablespoons apple cider vinegar

3 tablespoons baking powder

1 tablespoon ground cinnamon

1/2 teaspoon salt

Directions

Preheat a waffle iron according to manufacturer's instructions.

Mix flour, water, coconut oil, sugar, apple cider vinegar, baking powder, cinnamon, and salt together in a bowl until batter is smooth.

Ladle batter into the waffle iron and cook according to manufacturer's instructions until crisp, about 5 minutes.

Chapter 2: Vegan Lunch Recipes

Hot and Sour Soup

Ingredients

1 ounce dried wood ear mushrooms

4 dried shiitake mushrooms

12 dried tiger lily buds

2 cups hot water

1/3 ounce bamboo fungus

3 tablespoons soy sauce

5 tablespoons rice vinegar

1/4 cup cornstarch

1 (8 ounce) container firm tofu, cut into 1/4 inch strips

1 quart vegetable broth

1/4 teaspoon crushed red pepper flakes

1/2 teaspoon ground black pepper

3/4 teaspoon ground white pepper

1/2 tablespoon chili oil

1/2 tablespoon sesame oil

1 green onion, sliced

1 cup Chinese dried mushrooms

Directions

In a small bowl, place wood mushrooms, shiitake mushrooms, and lily buds in 1 1/2 cups hot water. Soak 20 minutes, until rehydrated. Drain, reserving liquid. Trim stems from the mushrooms, and cut into thin strips. Cut the lily buds in half.

In a separate small bowl, soak bamboo fungus in 1/4 cup lightly salted hot water. Soak about 20 minutes, until rehydrated. Drain, and mince.

In a third small bowl, blend soy sauce, rice vinegar, and 1 tablespoon cornstarch. Place 1/2 the tofu strips into the mixture.

In a medium saucepan, mix the reserved mushroom and lily bud liquid with the vegetable broth. Bring to a boil, and stir in the wood mushrooms, shiitake mushrooms, and lily buds. Reduce heat, and simmer 3 to 5 minutes. Season with red pepper, black pepper, and white pepper.

In a small bowl, mix remaining cornstarch and remaining water. Stir into the broth mixture until thickened.

Mix soy sauce mixture and remaining tofu strips into the saucepan. Return to boil, and stir in the bamboo fungus, chili oil, and sesame oil. Garnish with green onion to serve.

Corn Chowder

Ingredients

2 tablespoons olive oil

1 small onion, chopped

1 cup celery, chopped

1 cup carrots, chopped

1 clove garlic, minced

2 1/2 cups water

2 cubes vegetable bouillon

2 cups corn

2 cups soy milk

1 tablespoon flour

1 teaspoon dried parsley

1 teaspoon garlic powder

1 teaspoon salt

1 teaspoon pepper

Directions

Heat oil in a large skillet over medium heat. Stir in onions and celery; cook until just slightly golden. Stir in carrots and garlic; cook until garlic is slightly golden.

Meanwhile, bring water to a boil over high heat. Stir in bouillon, and reduce heat to medium. When bouillon cubes have dissolved, add corn and the vegetables from the skillet.

Cook until vegetables are tender. Add water, if necessary. Reduce heat to low, and pour in 1 cup soy milk. Stir soup well, then stir in remaining 1 cup soy milk. Quickly whisk in flour.

Stir in parsley, garlic powder, salt, and pepper. Cook, stirring constantly, until chowder thickens, about 15 to 20 minutes.

Beet And Carrot Salad

Ingredients

1 large beet, peeled and julienned

1 large carrot , peeled and julienned

1 clove garlic, minced finely

1 tbsp red onion, minced finely

2 tbsp fresh basil, slice in thin ribbons

4 tbsp fat free Italian dressing

Directions

Peel and julienne beet and carrot into a bowl. Mince onion and garlic, add to the bowl, and add basil to the bowl.

Toss with the dressing.

Black Bean Soup

Ingredients

1 tablespoon olive oil

1 large onion, chopped

1 stalk celery, chopped

2 carrots, chopped

4 cloves garlic, chopped

2 tablespoons chili powder

1 tablespoon ground cumin

1 pinch black pepper

4 cups vegetable broth

4 (15 ounce) cans black beans

1 (15 ounce) can whole kernel corn

1 (14.5 ounce) can crushed tomatoes

Directions

Heat oil in a large pot over medium-high heat. Saute onion, celery, carrots and garlic for 5 minutes.

Season with chili powder, cumin, and black pepper; cook for 1 minute. Stir in vegetable broth, 2 cans of beans, and corn. Bring to a boil.

Meanwhile, in a food processor or blender, process remaining 2 cans beans and tomatoes until smooth. Stir into boiling soup mixture, reduce heat to medium, and simmer for 15 minutes.

Chickpea Skillet

Ingredients

14 oz can chickpeas (garbanzo beans)

1 tbsp olive oil

14 oz can tomatoes

1 large onion, sliced

1 tbsp curry powder

2 tbsp smooth peanut butter

1 small box (1.5 oz) raisins

1/2 cup unsweetened apple juice

Directions

In a skillet sauté onion in olive oil.

Add chickpeas, curry, canned tomatoes, peanut butter, raisins and apple juice and cook for about 15 minutes.

Chunky Vegan Chili

Ingredients

1 tablespoon olive oil

1 onion, chopped

2 red bell pepper, seeded and chopped

1 jalapeno pepper, seeded and minced

10 fresh mushrooms, quartered

6 roma (plum) tomatoes, diced

1 cup fresh corn kernels

1 teaspoon ground black pepper

1 teaspoon ground cumin

1 tablespoon chili powder

2 (15 ounce) cans black beans, drained and rinsed

1 1/2 cups vegetable broth

1 teaspoon salt

Directions

Heat oil in a large saucepan over medium-high heat. Saute the onion, red bell peppers, jalapeno, mushrooms, tomatoes and corn for 10 minutes or until the onions are translucent.

Season with black pepper, cumin, and chili powder. Stir in the black beans, chicken or vegetable broth, and salt. Bring to a boil.

Reduce heat to medium low.

Remove 1 1/2 cups of the soup to food processor or blender; puree and stir the bean mixture back into the soup. Serve hot by itself or over rice.

Creamy Leek Soup

Ingredients

1 tablespoon extra-virgin olive oil

2 leeks, white and light green parts washed and sliced into 1/4-inch slices

2 cups chopped yellow onion

1/2 teaspoon sea salt

3 cloves garlic, minced

2 large Yukon Gold potatoes (about 1 pound), peeled and cubed into 1/2-inch cubes

4 cups vegetable stock

2-3 teaspoons fresh rosemary leaves

Directions

Heat a 4-quart soup pot over medium heat and add the oil.

Add the leeks, onion, and sea salt and saute for about 5 minutes, stirring often, until the onion begins to turn translucent.

Add the garlic and stir well. Cook for 1 minute more.

Add the potatoes and vegetable stock, cover, and bring to a boil. Reduce heat to simmer. Cook 20 minutes.

Remove the soup from the heat and use an immersion/stick blender to blend the soup in the pot or ladle the soup into a blender, 1 cup at a time. Blend the soup with the fresh rosemary leaves until smooth and free of chunks. Pour smooth soup into a heat-proof bowl and continue until all of the soup has been blended.

Transfer the blended soup back to the original soup pot and warm over low heat until heated through. Serve hot.

Vegan Bean Casserole

Ingredients

1 cup chickpeas

1 cup pinto beans

1 cup kidney beans

1/2 large onion

3 cloves garlic, chopped

1 cup red bell peppers, thinly sliced

10 pitted black olives, chopped

2 cans tomatoes

2 table spoon tomato puree

1/2 teaspoon salt

Dash of soy sauce

Black pepper

Fresh basil

1 bay leaf

Directions

In a large saucepan add olive oil and saute the onion, then add the garlic.

Add the peppers and olives into the pan. Saute for 5 minutes stirring all the time. Next add all of the Beans and cook for a further 10 minutes stirring occasionally making sure the beans don't stick to the bottom. Add both cans of tomatoes, the tomato paste, salt, soy sauce and bay leaf, place a lid over the saucepan.

Simmer on a low heat for an 1 hour, stirring every 10 minutes. 10 minutes before cooking time is finished add chopped fresh basil.

Quinoa Salad

Ingredients

1 cup quinoa

2 cups water

1/4 cup extra-virgin olive oil

2 limes, juiced

2 teaspoons ground cumin

1 teaspoon salt

1/2 teaspoon red pepper flakes, or more to taste

1 1/2 cups halved cherry tomatoes

1 (15 ounce) can black beans, drained and rinsed

5 green onions, finely chopped

1/4 cup chopped fresh cilantro

salt and ground black pepper to taste

Directions

Bring quinoa and water to a boil in a saucepan. Reduce heat to medium-low, cover, and simmer until quinoa is tender and water has been absorbed, 10 to 15 minutes. Set aside to cool.

Whisk olive oil, lime juice, cumin, 1 teaspoon salt, and red pepper flakes together in a bowl.

Combine quinoa, tomatoes, black beans, and green onions together in a bowl. Pour dressing over quinoa mixture; toss to coat. Stir in cilantro; season with salt and black pepper. Serve immediately or chill in refrigerator.

Chapter 3: Vegan Dinner Recipes

Savory Cabbage Casserole

Ingredients

4 cups cabbage, chopped/shredded

1/2 cup onion, diced

3 clove garlic, minced

28 oz can diced tomatoes

4 cups brown rice, cooked

2 tbsp vegan margarine

1/2 cup daiya vegan cheese

1/2 cup vegan bread crumbs

Directions

Ahead of time, cook brown rice to make 4 cups cooked rice.

In a little splash of oil, saute cabbage, onions, and garlic until onions are translucent. Once translucent, pour in the can of diced tomatoes. Season with salt and pepper to taste. Allow to simmer until flavors are well combined.

Preheat oven to 375 degrees. In a deep baking dish, lightly oil or spray the bottom of the dish and then spread half of the brown rice mixture into the bottom. Over the rice, spread half the cabbage mixture and then repeat.

In a small dish, heat the margarine until it's liquid. Mix this with the bread crumbs and the cheese until thoroughly combined.

Pour this over the cabbage mixture, which should be the top of the deep baking dish. Place dish into oven for 45 minutes.

Tofu And Vegetable Peanut Stir Fry

Ingredients

1 tablespoon peanut oil

1 small head broccoli, chopped

1 small red bell pepper, chopped

5 fresh mushrooms, sliced

1 pound firm tofu, cubed

1/2 cup peanut butter

1/2 cup hot water

2 tablespoons vinegar

2 tablespoons soy sauce

1 1/2 tablespoons molasses

ground cayenne pepper to taste

Directions

Heat oil in a large skillet or wok over medium-high heat. Saute broccoli, red bell pepper, mushrooms and tofu for 5 minutes.

In a small bowl combine peanut butter, hot water, vinegar, soy sauce, molasses and cayenne pepper. Pour over vegetables and tofu. Simmer for 3 to 5 minutes, or until vegetables are tender crisp.

Lentil Vegetable Bake

Ingredients

1/2 cup uncooked long grain white rice

2 1/2 cups water

1 cup red lentils

1 teaspoon vegetable oil

1 small onion, chopped

3 cloves garlic, minced

1 fresh tomato, chopped

1/3 cup chopped celery

1/3 cup chopped carrots

1/3 cup chopped zucchini

1 (8 ounce) can tomato sauce

1 teaspoon dried basil

1 teaspoon dried oregano

1 teaspoon ground cumin

salt and pepper to taste

Directions

Place the rice and 1 cup water in a pot, and bring to a boil. Cover, reduce heat to low, and simmer 20 minutes. Place lentils in a pot with the remaining 1 1/2 cups water, and bring to a boil. Cook 15 minutes, or until tender.

Preheat oven to 350 degrees F (175 degrees C).

Heat the oil in a skillet over medium heat, and stir in the onion and garlic. Mix in tomato, celery, carrots, zucchini, and 1/2 the tomato sauce. Season with 1/2 the basil, 1/2 the oregano, 1/2 the cumin, salt, and pepper. Cook until vegetables are tender.

In a casserole dish, mix the rice, lentils, and vegetables. Top with remaining tomato sauce, and sprinkle with remaining basil, oregano, and cumin.

Bake 30 minutes in the preheated oven, until bubbly.

Eggplant And Zucchini Stew

Ingredients

1 eggplant, cut into 1 inch cubes

1/4 cup olive oil

1 cup chopped onion

5 cloves garlic, chopped

1/2 cup Basmati rice

1 zucchini, cut into large chunks

1 large red bell pepper, chopped

3 fresh tomatoes, diced

1 cup Marsala wine

1 1/2 cups water

1/2 teaspoon salt, or to taste

1/4 teaspoon red pepper flakes

1/4 cup chopped fresh basil

1/4 cup chopped fresh parsley

1 sprig fresh rosemary, chopped

Directions

Place eggplant in a colander and sprinkle with salt.

Heat olive oil in a Dutch oven or large pot. Rinse eggplant and pat dry. Saute until slightly browned. Stir in onion and saute until transparent. Stir in garlic and saute for 2 to 3 minutes.

Stir in rice, zucchini, red bell pepper, tomatoes, wine, water, salt and red pepper flakes. Cook over medium-high heat until mixture reaches a low boil. Reduce heat and simmer for 45 minutes, or until vegetables are tender.

Remove from heat and stir in basil, parsley and rosemary.

Spicy Tofu Stir Fry

Ingredients

3 tablespoons peanut oil

1 pound firm tofu, cubed

1 red onion, sliced

1 red bell pepper, sliced

1 green chile pepper, chopped

3 cloves garlic, crushed

1/3 cup hot water

3 tablespoons white vinegar

3 tablespoons soy sauce

1 tablespoon brown sugar

1 teaspoon cornstarch

1 teaspoon crushed red pepper flakes

Directions

Heat peanut oil in a wok or large frying pan over medium-high heat. Toss the tofu into the oil, and cook until browned on all sides.

Once browned, toss in onion, bell pepper, chile pepper, and garlic; cook until just tender, about 5 minutes.

In a small bowl, whisk together the hot water, vinegar, soy sauce, brown sugar, cornstarch, and red pepper flakes. Pour over tofu and vegetables, toss to coat, and simmer 3 to 5 minutes, or until sauce thickens slightly.

Spinach Casserole

Ingredients

1 cup dry black-eyed peas

1/4 cup olive oil

1 onion, chopped

3 cups fresh spinach

1 (28 ounce) can peeled and diced tomatoes

2 teaspoons salt

1 teaspoon fennel seed, ground

Directions

Preheat oven to 350 degrees F (175 degrees C).

Cook black-eye peas in a pressure cooker for 12 minutes.

Heat oil in a large saucepan over medium high heat. Saute onion with spinach, tomatoes, salt and fennel for 15 minutes.

Combine beans with spinach mixture in a 2 quart casserole dish.

Bake in preheated oven for 15 minutes.

Squash Stir Fry

Ingredients

1 tablespoon olive oil, or as needed

3 cloves garlic, minced

1 yellow squash, cut into bite-size cubes

1 zucchini, cut into bite-size cubes

1 (12 ounce) package extra-firm tofu, cut into bite-size cubes

1/4 cup brown sugar

3 tablespoons soy sauce

1 tablespoon sriracha sauce

salt and ground black pepper to taste

Directions

Heat olive oil in a large skillet or wok over medium-high heat. Cook and stir garlic in hot oil until just fragrant, about 30 seconds. Add squash and zucchini, cook and stir until vegetables soften, about 7 minutes. Transfer squash mixture to a bowl.

Place skillet back over medium-high heat, place tofu pieces in the skillet, and top with brown sugar and soy sauce. Cook and stir until each side of tofu is golden brown, 3 to 5 minutes.

Return squash mixture to the skillet; cook and stir until heated through, about 3 minutes.

Stir in Sriracha sauce and season with salt and black pepper.

Asian Tofu Stir-Fry

Ingredients

1 (16 ounce) package firm tofu, cut into 3 slices

1 cup low-sodium soy sauce, divided

1 (1 inch) piece ginger, finely grated

1 tablespoon canola oil

1 yellow onion, sliced

1 large green bell pepper, cut into chunks

2 small zucchini, chopped

6 small mushrooms, chopped

3 tablespoons rice wine vinegar

1 tablespoon Asian hot-chile sauce

2 tablespoons crushed roasted peanuts

Directions

Lay tofu slices on a paper towel-lined plate and cover with more paper towels. Put a heavy object on top to press out excess water, about 15 minutes; drain and discard the accumulated liquid.

Mix 1/2 cup soy sauce and ginger in a large dish. Add tofu slices and let marinate, about 15 minutes.

Preheat oven to 350 degrees F (175 degrees C). Line a baking sheet with parchment paper.

Flip tofu slices and let marinate on second side, about 15 minutes more. Remove tofu from marinade and place on prepared baking sheet.

Bake in the preheated oven until dry, flipping once halfway through, about 40 minutes. Cut into smaller pieces.

Heat oil in a wok or large skillet over medium-high heat. Add onion and green bell pepper; cook until onion is slightly translucent, 3 to 5 minutes. Add zucchini and mushrooms; cook and stir until lightly browned, 2 to 3 minutes. Stir in baked tofu.

Mix remaining 1/2 cup soy sauce, rice wine vinegar, and chile sauce in a small bowl. Pour into the wok and stir until onion and tofu mixture is well-coated, about 1 minute. Garnish with roasted peanuts.

Slow Cooker Vegan Chili

Ingredients

1 tablespoon olive oil

1 green bell pepper, chopped

1 red bell pepper, chopped

1 yellow bell pepper, chopped

2 onions, chopped

4 cloves garlic, minced

1 (10 ounce) package frozen chopped spinach, thawed and drained

1 cup frozen corn kernels, thawed

1 zucchini, chopped

1 yellow squash, chopped

6 tablespoons chili powder

1 tablespoon ground cumin

1 tablespoon dried oregano

1 tablespoon dried parsley

1/2 teaspoon salt

1/2 teaspoon ground black pepper

2 (14.5 ounce) cans diced tomatoes with juice

1 (15 ounce) can black beans, rinsed and drained

1 (15 ounce) can garbanzo beans, drained

1 (15 ounce) can kidney beans, rinsed and drained

2 (6 ounce) cans tomato paste

1 (8 ounce) can tomato sauce, or more if needed

1 cup vegetable broth, or more if needed

Directions

Heat olive oil in a large skillet over medium heat, and cook the green, red, and yellow bell peppers, onions, and garlic until the onions start to brown, 8 to 10 minutes.

Place the mixture into a slow cooker. Stir in spinach, corn, zucchini, yellow squash, chili powder, cumin, oregano, parsley, salt, black pepper, tomatoes, black beans, garbanzo beans, kidney beans, and tomato paste until thoroughly mixed. Pour the tomato sauce and vegetable broth over the ingredients.

Set the cooker on Low, and cook until all vegetables are tender, 4 to 5 hours.

Check seasoning; if chili is too thick, add more tomato sauce and vegetable broth to desired thickness. Cook an additional 1 to 2 hours to blend the flavors.

Printed in Great Britain
by Amazon